FRASERBURGH

at

'WAR'

and the

'CORONATION'

an album of photographs and descriptions

compiled by
George Allan Dey
3, Maconochie Road, Fraserburgh,
ABERDEENSHIRE, AB43 8TH

designed by
Aberdeenshire Council Leisure and Recreation Department

printed by
BPC-AUP ABERDEEN Ltd.
Altens Industrial Estate
ABERDEEN AB1 4LE

ISBN 0 9512242 4 7

preface

PART 1: WAR

When I was halfway through preparing a book of historical interest around Fraserburgh, there arose considerable correspondence in the local 'Fraserburgh Herald' concerning the last war and the bombing of the town, much of which was confused and misleading, so I thought that it was time that a true record of events was put on record for posterity.

In order to make the story as accurate as possible, I researched the 'Police Records', the 'First Aid Post Records' and the 'Census Papers' and interviewed many people, and found that, although there were some slight differences in stories, there was enough to make a clear picture of what happened in Fraserburgh and Rosehearty during the 2nd World War.

I hope that what I have put together will give a clear indication of the devastating damage and suffering endured by all concerned.

PART 2: CORONATION

In part 2 there is a complete coverage of the 'Crowning' celebrations of the Queen in 1953 at Fraserburgh, The weather was dreadful - gales and rain - but that did not bother anyone except myself because of the difficulties of getting photographs.

With the improved printing papers now available, the pictures have come out better that expected 43 years after they were taken. Most of the young people in the parade will be parents now or even grand-parents and I am sure that they and their children will find the pictures of great interest. All the photographs in this section were taken by the author and are covered by copyright.

acknowledgements

Finally, I would like to give my sincere thanks to my many good friends who have helped me with information and identifications. Thanks also to 'Aberdeen Journals' for the use of wartime photographs and to the Aberdeenshire Council Leisure and Recreation Department for their help with designing the book.

George A. Dey

'WAR'

Some of the girls, directed from all over Aberdeenshire to the Fraserburgh 'Toolworks', who helped to win the war by making precision parts for the Rolls Royce Merlin engines used in the 'Spitfire' and 'Hurricane' fighter planes and 'Lancaster' bombers.

Back Row: Mary Barclay, Madgie Muirhead, Alice Stephen, Grace McPherson, Mary Cruden, Irene Duncan, Irene McCormack, Evelyn Ritchie, Eleanor McNab.

Next Row: Cathie Pirie, Jeannie Stephen, Jean Whyte, Dolly Johnstone, Netta Watt, Margaret Buchan, Bunty Bannerman, Elsie Strachan, Ella Jamieson, Hanna Monehan

Next Row: Ann Moffat, Chrissie Johnstone, Margaret Gunn, Eva Scott, Nellie Livingstone, Margaret Wood, Cathie Gibb, Ella Whyte, Lily Duthie, Chrissie Masson, Agnes Milne, Miss Pirie (cook), Sophie Buchan (secretary)

Next Row: Mabel Patterson, Betty Simpson, Nessie Turrel, Joan Fisher, Bella Cowe, Mary Watt, Helen McGaw, Violet Lunnan, Helen Marr, Chrissie Doig, Mary Yeats, Gladys Massie, Fenella Dick, Helen Mowat, Beth McHardy, Babs Shirron,

Next Row: Winnie Brown, Bella Lee, Helen Carle, Betty Reid, Katie Murdoch, Alexzena Hepburn, Edna Murison, Chrissie Murison, Annie Wallace, Margaret Gauld, Memmie Scott

Front Row: Betty Ironside, Rhea Sim, Olive Carle, Edith Colvin, Chrissie McNab, Sheila Noble

The BEGINNING of FLYING

As the first part of this book deals with bombing attacks by enemy flying machines on Fraserburgh during the 2nd World War in 1939 to 1945, it may be of interest at the outset to mention briefly the development of flying machines and the only two bombing incidents which happened in Scotland during the First World War.

The first recorded flight of an aeroplane in the Highlands occurred on the 24th June 1912, when a single wing aeroplane (known as a monoplane) called the 'Firefly' sponsored by the Daily Mail and piloted by a Mr B.C. Hucks, landed and was displayed at the games at Strathpeffer, a short distance from Cromarty Firth. There must have been some significance behind this flight as will be noted in the next incident.

In the summer of 1913 (a year later), the first aeroplane seen at Fraserburgh landed on the links. It was a 'Farnham' two wing (biplane) type and, curiously, if we had seen it flying today, we would have thought that it was flying backwards because the pilot sat at the "tail" end looking over the tail wing and with the engine and large wings behind him.

It was flown by Capt. Dawes from Montrose and stopped at various places including Keith on August 1913 and then at Nairn. It was probably one from a group of 'Farnham' aircraft which were flown to Cromarty Firth a year before World War I by members of the 'Naval Wing' of the 'Royal Flying Corps', who were looking for an air base suitable for use by 'Farnham' seaplanes. These aircraft had the engines at the front where we would expect them to be.

When they were at Nairn they had probably been looking at the large Findhorn Bay beside which is the present R.A.F. air field.

The base established at Cromarty eventually proved to be an ideal place for use by large Sunderland flying boats during World War II.

The first aeroplane flight in the Highlands at the Strathpeffer games,
August 14th 1912, with the Daily Mail 'Firefly'. The start of a flight.

The pilot Mr B.C. Hucks is standing in front of the propeller and beside him is the manager
along with mechanics and local handymen.

This is the 'Farnham' aeroplane which landed on Fraserburgh links beside the putting green in 1913. The plane was piloted by Captain Dawes, seen on the extreme left. It was reported later seen at Keith and Nairn.

George Dean's aeroplane nearly completed at Invernorth, Rathen 1911. The people in the picture **L to R:** Wm. Park, John Scott (Crimond), George Morrice, Robt. Park and George Dean with parts of the aeroplane laid out on the ground. The propellers were passed on to the Fraserburgh A.T.C. Personally, I think that the blades were too wide at the tips for efficiency.

Strangely enough, there could have been an even earlier flight at Fraserburgh if an ambitious man had finished building an aeroplane, but he had to leave the district in a hurry before completing it.

The project began in 1911 when the Daily Mail offered a prize of £1,000 for the first flight between Glasgow and Edinburgh in a Scottish built aircraft. This offer came to the notice of two ex-Buchan men, George Morrice and John Scott, who were then living in America. Teaming up with an Englishman George Dean they started work at the premises of W. & R. Park, coach builders and wheelwrights at Invernorth, Rathen near Fraserburgh, where Morrice had served his apprenticeship.

Their plan was to build an aircraft described as a Racing Bi-Plane - 20ft by 22ft with a 60 horse power engine giving a speed of 86 m.p.h. at 870 revs per min. Morrice and Scott concentrated on the airframe while Dean worked on the engine. As none of them could fly, they found a pilot from Nelson, Lancashire, with the unfortunate name of Bert Nutter.

The work suddenly came to an end when Dean heard that his wife, whom he had deserted, was heading north to look for him, so he promptly disappeared and abandoned his aeroplane.

There is a story that he was so keen on flying that when the war started in 1914 he joined the Royal Flying Corps, but was unfortunately killed when on active service.

THE FIRST "BOMBING" IN SCOTLAND 3RD MAY 1916

'Craig Castle' near Lumsden, Aberdeenshire

Coming back to the two bombing incidents - these were not carried out by aeroplanes but by German Zeppelins (airships).

On the night of 2nd/3rd May 1916, eight Zeppelins set off to attack Rosyth and the Forth Bridge but, scattered by gales, only two reached Scotland and, of these, one, the 'LI4', dropped its bombs on the lights of a fishing fleet off Arbroath believing he was over the Firth of Forth - they exploded harmlessly.

The 'L2O', commanded by Kaptainleutnant Franz Stabbert, crossed the Scottish coast north of Arbroath with snow and fog making navigation very difficult.

It then arrived at Deeside passing over Glen Clunie Lodge, Inverey, and Derry Lodge before flying on to Aviemore - it then turned east over Aberdeenshire at the Strathdon area and bombed Craig Castle, which was brilliantly lit up by its own generating plant that night for a social gathering. It carried on eastward dropping bombs on farmland around Insch and Old Rayne before it left crossing the coast between Newburgh and Peterhead.

The 'L2O' never got back to its base because it was wrecked when it made a forced landing in a fjord near Stavanger. Kaptainleutnant Stabbert and nine of his crew were interned and six others repatriated.

I can confirm that a bomb was dropped at the Castle because, when I visited the castle on business in 1933, the Laird came with me to the front door when I had finished and, pointing to the beautiful lawn on the other side of the drive, he said, "Do you see that hole in the lawn - well - that was made by a bomb dropped from a Zeppelin in 1916 and I never filled it in but left it as an unusual souvenir of the War."

After I had written that, I decided that I would go to the Castle, 70 miles from home, and try to get a suitable picture to illustrate the story. When I got there, I met the present owner, Mr Barcas, who said that he was the grandson of the man I had met in 1933. He did not know the position of the hole in the lawn - it had been filled in - but he gave me proof of the event by producing a rather faded photograph of the remains of the bomb lying in the hole, which I promptly copied. I also photographed the Castle with the lawn in front and both pictures now appear with this story.

Further Comments about Zeppelins and Airships

During the 1st World War, Zeppelin bombing attacks occurred frequently over London and towns up the east coast. As there were no fighter airplanes available at that time to attack them, the only means of defence was by the use of guns. In Aberdeen, there was battery of guns at the beach links where shooting practice went on almost every day: the method of operation was for one gun to fire a shell high into the sky which exploded in a ball of white smoke as a simulated target which the other guns aimed at when firing shells of black smoke.

When I was about 8 years old (80 years ago) and lived in the Mile End district of Aberdeen I used to watch how well they performed not really knowing what it was all about. But, when I started writing about airship attacks the other day, it all came clear to me. I have been informed that the famous 'Graf Zeppelin' passenger ship passed over Fraserburgh, then over Aberdeen in 1930, where I saw it pass over the harbour and fly eastwards. The Germans had another large airship the 'Hindenburg' which, unfortunately, met with a terrible disaster after a flight to America in 1937. It was always necessary when the ships arrived at an airport to have a large squad of men available to catch and hold on to ropes dropped down to them to manoeuvre the ships into position for unloading. On this occasion, when the ropes reached the ground there was a bright flash, thought to have been static electricity, which travelled up the ropes and caused an explosion. It ripped through the airship which was full of highly explosive hydrogen gas and killed all on Board and some ground crew. After that the Germans stopped using Zeppelins a name which they were called after their inventor Count Zeppelin.

There is news now that they are starting to build a re-designed aircraft filled with helium non-explosive gas and using a steering system with propellers and engines which can be swivelled to guide the ship in any direction - a sort of power steering. This was an invention by a British firm 'Airship Industries' which made the small airships seen on T.V. at sports events and used for advertising, but who received no industrial support and had to close down. In closing, I must mention that, during the 1st World War, home-made airships were made and used at Longside airport near Peterhead. These were very useful for patrolling and spotting German submarines around the Buchan coast. Full details and stories may be found in Jim Buchan's book 'Bygone Buchan', which was published a few years ago.

The remains of the bomb lying in the hole in the Castle lawn.

The Zeppelin L20 ditched off the Norwegian coast after the Scottish raid on 3rd May 1916.

A 'Zeppelin' (airship) flying over Leipzig in Germany from a postcard dated 18th December 1913. This was the forerunner of war type Zeppelins used against Britain, particularly London, during the 1st World War.

This is the German 'Graf Zeppelin' seen at Fraserburgh then at Aberdeen where I saw it flying over the harbour in 1930 on its way to Germany via the North Sea.

The Hindenberg explosion, in 1937 in New Jersey, USA. Germany stopped using airships after this disaster.

The 1st WORLD WAR - 1914 *to* 1918

1914. Men being called up for service at the start of the war. Town council officials on the stairway of the Dalrymple Cafe' include Mr Anderson, J. Finlayson and Mr A. Gordon.
Copied from a postcard on the back of which is written "They fought for King and Country for 1 shilling (5p) a day". It is a rather sad picture because many never returned.

Spectators outside the Dalrymple Hall watching the men being photographed in 1914.

Soldiers marching down Victoria street passing what used to be the Bellsea Hotel, now a car showroom, on their way to the railway station for transport to France at the start of the First World War on 4th August 1914. They had just been kitted out at the Fraserburgh Drill Hall in Grattan Place.

Two days before the War was declared on the 4th August 1914, 257 naval reservists got their "call up papers" and, watched by a large crowd at the harbour, they were paraded and marched to the railway station where they boarded a train and by 3.30 pm they were on their way to Portsmouth. Another 230 went on the following day.

1916. During the First World War, Winston Churchill toured the country promoting war bonds, saving certificates, etc. using one of the first made British tanks as a platform. It is said to be him in this picture but it is most unlikely that he would have travelled up to this North East corner of Scotland. Of the other men on the tank the one on the right travelled with the promoter and beside him, I think, is Major J. Reach, Councillor and Banker, and on the left possibly Mr A. Anderson, both of Fraserburgh.

The German troops were tremendously shocked when they saw these tanks rolling towards them when they were first used.

I include the next two photographs taken in July 1926 because they complement the statements in Mr Bill McDonald's book about Fraserburgh Harbour that large numbers of fishing boats, patrol boats and mine sweepers etc were sunk by mines all round our coasts. For years after the war, in spite of regular minesweeping operations, there were still mines floating about or lying on the sea floor making trawl fishing a very hazardous operation.

You may wonder how I got this photograph. Well - at that time I had nearly finished serving my time as a ship draughtsman at A. Hall & Co's shipyard in Aberdeen. Being curious to know how all the gear was used on an Aberdeen trawler, I got the opportunity to spend my one week holiday two years in succession on the trawler the 'Danella'. On this, my second trip, we were trawling about 100 miles east of Fraserburgh and getting good catches when, suddenly, the fishermen thought the net had caught on to something. The boat was stopped and the net slowly pulled up and it was then that we saw a mine at the cod end of the net.

It was gently lowered on to the fore deck and the net cut away and it was then that we saw a dent in the mine in a space between the "horn" detonators which showed that it had been struck by a ship, fortunately not on a detonator, and had dropped to the seabed. There was nothing we could do except pack up and return to Aberdeen where it was disposed of near the mouth of the Don.

I plucked up the courage to take the photograph and then spent the time anxiously on the way back sitting at the aft end beside their lifeboat (a dinghy). If the mine had exploded you wouldn't be reading this story.

The Danella's first catch of the day.

The second catch of the day! A German mine picked up in the trawl net of the
Aberdeen trawler 'Danella' 100 miles east of Fraserburgh in 1926.

FRASERBURGH WAR MEMORIAL

The assembly at the square of the various organisations which included members and officials of the Town Council, Harbour Commissioners, Feuars' Managers, Customs and Excise, Parish Council, Coastguards, the Boys' Brigade, the Girl Guides, Officers of Solomon Lodge of Freemasons and the Fraserburgh Lodge of Freemasons, the Free Gardeners, the Oddfellows, the Shepherds, the I.O.G.T., who all then marched down to the Memorial.

This shows a 'guard of honour' to Sir Ian Hamilton, the Colonel of the Gordon Highlanders as he approached the Memorial between two lines of ex-soldiers and ex-sailors, all wearing their medals and all under the command of Captain the Master of Saltoun, M.C., who can be seen in uniform at the end of the right hand row. It is a particularly sad reflection that his son (brother of the present Lady Saltoun), who was killed in the 1939-45 War, has his name engraved on one of the four corner panels added to the memorial just after the last War. The face beside the 'top hat' is that of Sir Ian Hamilton.

UNVEILING DAY SCENES - 9TH SEPTEMBER 1923

As he unveiled the War Memorial, Sir Ian Hamilton declared, "To the Glory of God and in the memory of the heroes of Fraserburgh, I unveil this memorial." He then stood to attention and saluted the Memorial as did the entire company, whilst buglers Pressley and Mitchell sounded the 'Last Post'. On the right of Sir Ian can be seen, in the black suit, Joe Watt V.C., and on his left, Mr John Carle representing the Sea Forces. On the other side of the Memorial were Mr James Milne and Mr Leslie representing the Military Forces.

Sir Ian Hamilton (on the platform on the left of the picture) then addressed the assembly and thanked Provost Brown for inviting him to the ceremony. He said he was proud, as any Scotsman would be, to take part in the same ceremony with two of the men there - Joseph Watt V.C. and Lt-Col. Samuel McDonald. Provost Brown presided at the ceremony and, amongst those on the platform including Sir Ian, were Lord Saltoun, Lt. Col. Kelly, Col. Forbes C.M.G., ex Provost Finlayson, Rev. J.H. Williams, West Church, sitting nearest to the Memorial, and the ministers of all the local churches. Amongst the general company present were the Hon. Mrs A.A. Fraser, Philorth House, Mrs Brown and Mrs Webster, who were wearing their decorations gained while on active service as nurses. It was estimated that over 6,000 people, including the massed local church choirs attended the ceremony in memory of the 411 men who lost their lives in the First World War. Captain the Master of Saltoun is seen below Rev. Williams.

Members of the Fraserburgh ex-Servicemen's Club, 1914-1918 War: photograph c. 1935. **LtoR**
Back Row: Addison, Wright, A. Mair, J.C. Summers, J. Noble, A. Noble, J. Findlay, A. Colvin, A. Barclay, Watt, J. Milne
Next Row: J. McHardy, G.B. Walker, A. Davidson, J. McLeman, J. Barclay, F. McLauchlin, A. Watt, J. McMaster, J. Noble
Next Row: J. Fraser
Front Row: W. Duthie, J. Mitchell, H. Pressley, A McGee, Lord Saltoun, J. Sim (Brave), Joe Watt (V.C.), J. Carle, W. Ingram, S. Gordon

JOSEPH WATT, V.C.

The story about Joe Watt, seen in the adjoining picture, appears to be forgotten nowadays and now wonder, because the incident which earned him the Victoria Cross happened 80 years ago, during the First World War.

Joe, born at Gamrie in 1889, became skipper of the fishing boat 'Gowanlea' (FR 105) which was built by Scott & Yule Shipbuilders, Fraserburgh, in 1914 for John Strachan & Bros. of Inverallochy. The wooden boat of 87 feet keel was immediately commissioned for patrol and mine sweeping duties by the Admiralty and in due course was sent to the Adriatic where one night it was accosted by three light enemy cruisers who demanded their surrender.

Joe, with the support of his crew, opened fire with their 6lb gun against the cruisers and managed to evade them and get away safely. The gunner was a deckhand named Fred Lamb who, unfortuantely, had his leg shatterd by a shell. But that didn't stop him shooting until they got safely away. The other members of the crew were William Noble, A. Wilson and J. Murdoch.

In an earlier incident, Joe Watt was in his cabin when a shell passed right through it. The funnel was blown away and several of the crew were killed. The lifeboat with the ship's compass was lowered but, after some difficulty, he made contact with another patrol ship which, at first, thought it was an enemy ship because his boat was unrecognisable lacking its funnel.

His bravery was recognised by Sir John Jellicoe after which he was awarded the Victoria Cross and later he received the King of Serbia's Gold Medal for Bravery.

Lord Saltoun, seen in the photograph, also took part in the First War and, unfortunately, was captured and became a prisoner of war during which time he occupied himself with knitting socks.

Sadly, his son, brother of Lady Saltoun, was killed in the Second World War and his name can be seen on the corner panel facing up Saltoun Place on the War Memorial.

Another man in the photograph, George Bremner Walker, had the rather unpleasant experience of seeing his name on the Memorial amongst all those killed, which arose from an error in the information supplied which listed him as, "missing presumed dead". He survived for many years afterwards.

17

The 2nd WORLD WAR - 1939 *to* 1945

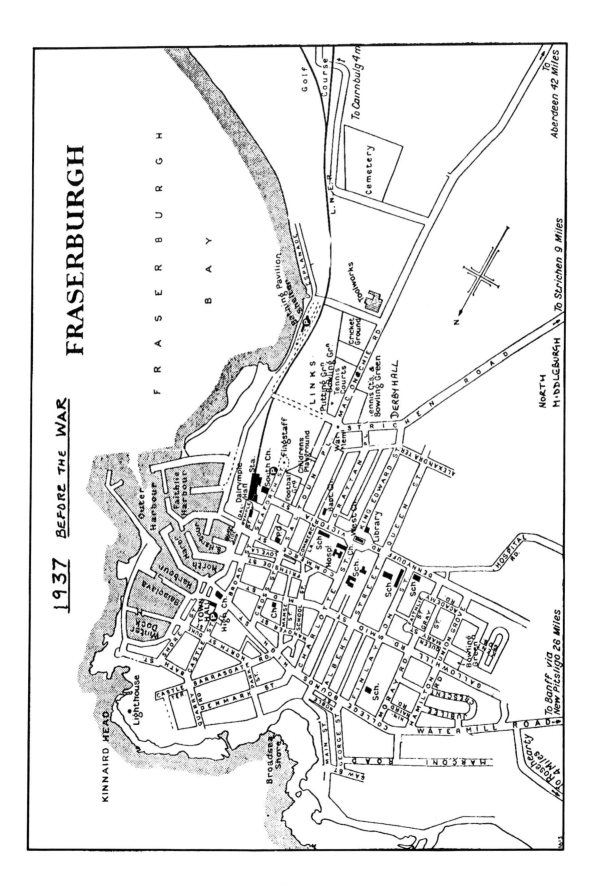

Map of Fraserburgh c. 1937.

At the outset of the War, little consideration was given to the possibility of attack by the German forces on the North East of Scotland. Consequently, there was very little in the way of defences apart from the Home Guard and a few machine guns. Following the defeat in France, the authorities set about establishing obstacles against possible landings:

1 Minefields were laid along the coast at all easy landing places - example; at the sandhole at the end of the "Prom".

2 Telephone type poles were 'planted' in all flat areas to obstruct the landing of gliders full of troops, towed across from Norway by bombers example; the Fraserburgh Playing Fields.

3 Masses of square concrete blocks were laid at all vulnerable places - example; at the beach caravan park.

4 Concrete defence 'Pill' boxes were positioned at all main road junctions and around factories - example; there is still one at the beach.

Fortunately there was no invasion, but Fraserburgh and district suffered intermittent bombing raids, usually without warning because the planes flew in too low to be detected by radar.

Only the Fraserburgh and district attacks are listed in this book but there were many attacks on shipping, especially on convoys where many ships were lost. Kinnaird Lighthouse was lit only when convoys were due to pass.

Air defence of the Fraserburgh area was covered by fighter aeroplanes from Longside or Banff but Fraserburgh airfield (as it was officially known) at Cairnbulg/Inverallochy was generally a training station. The first training

A view looking south across Fraserburgh bay, with Maconochie's food factory in the foreground.

planes were two-winged 'Sword Fish'. They were very slow moving and were first used on aircraft carriers and were at Fraserburgh for about one year. Then 'Oxford' monoplanes were in use up to near the end of the War. There was one unfortunate crash on the 24th May 1943 at Fraserburgh airfield when two planes tried to land at the same time, one above the other and unsighted, and two men were killed.

Now a word about living conditions in Fraserburgh during the War which started on Sunday the 3rd September 1939

Immediately War was declared, Fraserburgh had to prepare defences against air attack, so all premises and street lighting had to be blacked-out and all important factories had their roofs camouflaged with green and brown paints. Netting was draped over roofs where necessary. Churches were unsuitable for blacking out so services were confined to daylight.

All men under 40 not in reserved occupations were enrolled for duty in the various forces. All able bodied men in reserved occupations had to enrol for essential duties. Some were air raid wardens (who patrolled the streets checking that no lights were showing at night), others auxiliary Police and Fireman and in the Home Guard, whilst others had to train the younger people in organisations such as the Air Training Corps, the Sea Cadets and Girls' organisations. Other qualified people had to teach at evening schools to cover a shortage of teachers. Young women had to enrol for duty in factories and hospitals and work on farms.

Older women were expected to volunteer to help in canteens in church halls which were commissioned to cater for members of the forces and allies stationed in Fraserburgh district.

Rationing, of course, came into force and ration books were issued for food, clothing and petrol. Supplies of sugar in particular were very limited so sweets were scarce and rationed by the Government. No ice cream was made and wedding cakes had covers of cardboard made to look like icing.

Clothing was a problem. Old garments were cut down for children and woollen garments were ripped up to re-use the wool to make comforts for the forces. Coupons had to be given at church sales of work. Petrol rationing required coupons to be given up sufficient to allow approx 100 miles per month i.e. one trip to Aberdeen and back with a drop left over. With licence and insurance also to be paid for, it was not worth it, so most people laid up their cars. Farmers got petrol with a pink dye in it for use in their machinery, but if anyone was caught with it in a car they were prosecuted.

Most of the larger fishing boats were commissioned for use as mine sweepers or patrol boats but the smaller inshore boats were not required so a certain amount of fresh fish was available. Sometimes additional meat was obtainable in the butcher's when the fishing fleet moved south to East Anglia.

Some people were able to supplement their egg ration (often one egg per person per week) by buying eggs from farmers.

From the above you may think that life in wartime Fraserburgh was quite tolerable but, when you read all about the bombings, you will realise what a difficult time it was for the people of Fraserburgh.

FRASERBURGH AIRFIELD

As a follow up to the previous stories about aircraft it may be of interest to have a brief description of Fraserburgh Airfield as it was officially known, although it was actually located at Inverallochy/Cairnbulg.

Originally built as a satellite for Peterhead Airport it had three runways and five 'hurricane' pens each capable of accommodating two aircraft. It was officially opened on 6th December 1941 and the first aircraft to arrive were 'Swordfish' biplanes of 823 squadron, a type of plane normally used on aircraft carriers because of their slow take-off speed. Members of Fraserburgh air training corps had the privilege of getting flights in them and I and two cadets in a flight of three aeroplanes found it nice looking down over the sides of the open cockpits at Strathbeg and all around from about 3,000 feet up until the planes suddenly started diving and left our stomachs still up there. The cadets were rather green after it. It was a good experience all the same.

The aeroplane squadron was moved away, however, in May 1942 and, after a few changes, 'Oxford' training aircraft were brought in and stayed until the end of 1944 when it was taken over by Coastal Command who brought in 'Warwick' aircraft for air sea rescue duty, carrying lifeboats which were dropped by parachutes. The last to land at Fraserburgh was a 'Sea Fury' which had engine trouble and made an emergency landing safely on 9th September 1952.

THE FIRST AIR RAID AT FRASERBURGH

On the 16th July 1940 the first air raid on Fraserburgh occurred - a beautiful day with a clear sky and the beach crowded with women and children. At the toolworks, in the design office at the corner of Kessock Road, I was discussing a job with "Skipper" Andrew Noble, a First World War veteran, when suddenly just after 4pm we heard a shrill whistling noise. He turned to me immediately and said, "That's a bomb." The explosion that followed proved him right and, when we looked out of the window, we saw a large column of black smoke near the South Church.

"Go to your shelters," we were told and we ran to our designated shelter on the other side of the South Road. Within minutes terrified women and children came running up from the beach and they were all taken to the shelters and stayed there until we got the 'all clear'. Some of the women said that they heard the droning of an aircraft for some time before four bombs were dropped across the town and that no warning was given until after the bombs fell.

The first bomb landed near the bottom of Station Brae in the middle of the road between the Dalrymple Hall and the Railway Station (now the Job Centre). The explosion shattered the glass roof of the Station and also damaged the windows of the Station Hotel, The South Church and Hall.

The second bomb fell at the back of the tenement building No.20 Frithside Street and close to the back of the Royal Bank of Scotland which was badly damaged. The back of the tenement was completely stripped down and what was left of it soon fell down. A postman having an afternoon rest upstairs had a rude awakening and fortunately escaped serious injury.

The third bomb fell on a store between Hanover Street and the Co-op building in High Street. The fourth bomb fell at the back of the Alexandra Hotel in High Street. Much damage was done by these bombs and 36 people were injured.

Mr George Duncan, manager of The Royal Bank of Scotland in Broad Street, Fraserburgh, surveys the damage to tenement buildings in Frithside Street behind the bank where the second bomb fell.

Mr R.M. Nicoll, accountant at the Royal Bank of Scotland, looks at more destruction of the Frithside St. house behind the bank.

This picture shows the back of the Royal Bank of Scotland, Broad Street, which suffered serious bomb damage.

27-7-1940 Air raid at 'Toolworks'

On 27th July 1940 at 1.17am, a German plane passed over Fraserburgh and dropped 2 High Explosive (HE) bombs at Rosehearty at 1.20am. Five minutes later it approached Fraserburgh from the east and dropped 2 HE bombs on the sand dunes 300 yards east of the cemetery lodge. It again passed over the town at about 500 feet flying from south west to north east and released eight bombs - six in a field owned by Lord Saltoun and two in a Kirkton farm corn field. These bombs fell in practically a straight line, the last one falling 80 yards from the Toolworks. Window panes and roof slates of the toolworks and houses were damaged.

13-8-1940 Air raid - Harbour, Finlayson Street, Queen Mary Street, & W.E Bowling Green

At 10.45pm on 13th August 1940, an air attack was made on Fraserburgh when 17 bombs were dropped. The enemy aircraft came in from the east and dropped five bombs in the harbour where they exploded without doing any damage.

It carried on in a straight line and dropped a string of bombs at Finlayson Street beginning where the footpath goes through to Queen Mary Street, then hitting houses in Queen Mary Street, then across Union Grove and the West End bowling green and a field at the west of the green. I remember in particular the remains of a house at the top corner of Viewfield Road and Queen Mary Street - just the remnants of the roof of the house lying on a heap of rubble. Two council houses were destroyed and many others damaged. There were 16 casualties two of them later died from their injuries.

2-10-1940 Air raid - Percyhorner, Lochpots, Middleburgh, Strichen Road, Derbyhall, Playing Fields, Toolworks and Railway Line.

At 8.40pm on Wednesday 2nd October 1940, an enemy aircraft circled the town and then, coming in from the south west, it dropped a string of 12 HE bombs and then about 24 incendiary bombs. The first HE bombs fell in a grass field belonging to R&C Sutherland, farmers at Percyhorner, the next in a grassfield at the roadside, then four in fields at Lochpots, three at Middleburgh and Strichen Road and on a field at Derbyhall.

Incendiary bombs were then dropped over Derbyhall, the playing fields, on the Aberdeen Road at the junction with Kessock Road. Then one fell into a toolworks store beside Kessock Road, but fortunately none caused any damage.

There was no air raid alarm and I was astonished when I saw a burning incendiary on the road outside the drawing office. There were no casualties.

5-11-1940 Air raid - Benzies & Millers fire and commercial bar

At 7.05pm fire was reported to have broken out at the premises in Mid Street owned and occupied by Messrs. Benzie and Miller, drapers and household furnishers, and, as the fire got beyond the control of the local fire brigade, appliances had to be called in from outwith the town in an effort to subdue the fire which was raging furiously at 9.00pm.

An air raid warning was sounded at 7.25pm because raiders had been heard flying over the town attracted by the glare of the fire and at 9.16pm bombs were dropped.

One made a direct hit on the Commercial Bar, Kirk Brae, in the centre of the town and demolished it completely along with surrounding property. Sadly, a darts match was in progress in the bar in which 34 people were killed: 52 others there and in the area were injured.

A bus to Rosehearty standing near was also damaged, but not enough to stop it from fleeing to Rosehearty with a load of frightened people. But, unfortunately it was caught by the blast of another bomb which exploded in a field just as the bus was passing Gallowhill Terrace. It must have been a very large bomb for we felt the shock of it down at 25 College Bounds (Gracie Craigs) and, when I saw the bomb crater next day, it was deep and very wide. Fortunately, it was in an empty field, part of Corbet's farm.

There were many heroes in the town that night, particularly the firemen, who had to carry on fighting the many fires despite the risk of further bombing. All through the night and next day the Air Raid Precaution (ARP), soldiers and police had the heartbreaking job of digging the dead and injured out of the ruined buildings.

At 9.16pm the same night a bomb was dropped in the sea at Sandhaven causing slight damage to 2 houses at "Bells" buildings.

Next day on 6th Nov an unexploded bomb was found in the back garden of Nos. 22&24 Union Grove.

5th November 1940. Air raid during Benzie & Miller's fire.
The picture shows the Commercial Bar at the top of Kirk Brae, owned by Peter O'Hara, which was destroyed by a large bomb along with the houses on the right. Next door was the shop of Peter Bruce, a Butcher. Then, the entrance door to the houses above, then a Haberdashery shop occupied by Mrs West. The next building of two shops and house above was occupied by C. Marioni with a confectionary-chip shop and billiard saloon. The pillars of the entrance door and window can be seen beside Pressley's bakery shop.

5th November 1940. Fraserburgh's Worst Air Raid.

This clearly shows the immense destruction to the Commercial Bar and adjacent properties after a direct hit by a very large bomb. 34 people were killed and 52 injured.

5th November 1940.

This was all that was left of Marioni's shop and the end wall was so badly damaged that it collapsed on to the Bakery which had to be demolished and later re-built.

The "Commercial Bar" after some days of tidying up. Note the thickness of the wall on the right of this old building.

5th November 1940. Air raid at Gallowhill Terrace during the fire at Benzie & Miller's Store.
The picture shows the west end part of Fraserburgh at the end of Watermill Road and Gallowhill Terrace and some pre-fab houses built after the war. In the field, part of the Corbet's Farm, the last bomb of the raid was dropped approximately at the spot marked on the photograph and tremors from it were felt all over Broadsea and as far down as Charlotte Street. The hole in the field was very large and could have swallowed up one of the blocks of flats now standing there.

7-2-1941 AIR RAID - GASWORKS ETC.

At 11.40am on Friday 7th February 1941, a German plane flew along the coast from Rosehearty then moved inland towards Fraserburgh flying at less than 100 feet over Gallowhill road. My wife saw if from our house in College Bounds and thought it was having engine trouble because of the unusual popping noise it was making but discovered later that it was machine gunning all the way into town. She also saw two bombs drop as it went over the Gasworks: the first one fell between the two gas holders damaging the upright supports of one of them and causing some cracks in the tank from which some escaping gas caught fire. The pressure was immediately reduced and the fire extinguished with the help of the fire brigade.

The bomb, meantime, continued its path across a lane, then through a kippering kiln and part of the works, causing a lot of damage before it finally came to rest in an open yard at the corner of Albert Street without exploding. No one was injured, but if it had exploded at the Gasworks there would have been a major catastrophe and the plane itself could have been destroyed by the force of the explosion. The second bomb struck the chimney head of the house belonging to Mr and Mrs Greig at the corner of Mid Street and Charlotte Street, and it penetrated the roof, coming to rest in an upstairs scullery where it failed to explode. Mrs Greig received an injury to her ankle and was given first aid treatment at the Thomas Walker Hospital in Charlotte Street. The plane continued machine gunning right into the town. A 65 year old man, Mr Andrew Strachan of 1 Main Street, Inverallochy, was slightly wounded by a bullet which grazed his forehead and a horse belonging to Wordie the carrier was wounded in one leg. The bombs were of 500lbs, and there was no alert at the time.

This picture is included because it is the only one I could find which shows one of the two massive storage tanks at the 'Gasworks' near the corner of Mid Street and Finlayson Street. By a miracle, a German bomb passed through a small gap between the tanks causing only minor damage to the supporting structure and did not explode when it fell to the ground.

For those interested - the early Peugot Car RS21 is standing outside 'Williamson's' garage (now a Riteway store) and in the driving seat is Alex R. Walker with A. Williamson sitting beside him and behind Williamson is J. Cantley. Sitting on the footboard is R. Forsyth ("Pommer") and standing on left is W. Hepburn. The other two are not known. Note that the car lights are activated by acetylene (carbide) gas.

19-2-41 AIR RAID, CASTLE TERRACE AND QUARRY ROAD AREA

At 10.38am on Wednesday 19th February 1941, a low level attack was made on Fraserburgh by a single German plane. It approached the town from the south and passed over the Toolworks at a height of about 100 feet. It flew northwards straight across the links and, on reaching the town, rose to about 200 feet. As it crossed the harbour side of the town, it dropped two 1,000lb HE bombs.

One struck the middle of Castle Terrace, about 25 yards from its junction with Castle Street then bounced through a stone wall on the east side of the yard in Quarry Road occupied by Gordon & Co. Timber Merchants. Then it went through one of the A.R.P. mortuaries and exploded in the corner of the yard nearest to the sea. The second bomb fell and exploded about 15 yards further on from the first one. The plane then flew out to sea. The attack, which was carried out during an alert, seemed to be aimed at Maconochie's Factory which the plane flew over: the bombs missed their target by only a few yards. This factory would have been considered to be an important target because it produced rations for the armed forces. There were 15 people injured and about 30 properties were damaged.

5-4-1941 AIR RAID - MACONOCHIES FACTORY

At 10.43am on Saturday 5th April 1941, a single German plane, a Heinkel III, flew in over the north breakwater to make a low level attack on the factory.

Two 500lb bombs were dropped, the first one a few yards inside the road at the entrance gate where it exploded making a crater 6ft deep by 12ft wide. The second bomb landed in the kitchen area after tearing through the vegetable, stock preparing and meat departments, a distance of about 70 yards. Then it came to rest unexploded where about 100 women were working. In the understandable panic, a large number of the women were injured in their frantic efforts to escape through broken windows and doors. The air raid warning was received at 10.44am, one minute after the bombs were dropped. All services were quickly mobilized, including a first aid team (myself included) from the toolworks and all casualties were removed to the first aid post by 12.15pm. Twenty one of the casualties with injuries requiring surgery were taken to Aberdeen. There was a total of 126 injured and six killed. There was considerable damage to the factory consisting of 5,600 sq. ft. in the kitchen area and 4,500 sq. ft. of the dye room and the boiler was seriously damaged. Damage also was caused to about 80 private properties, houses and shops, mostly to roofs and windows.

17-4-1941 AIR RAID - CASTLE STREET

At 3.22pm on the 17th April 1941, a German plane flew in low from the north and passed along Quarry Road and turned towards Castle Street, where it fired its machine guns and also dropped two 500lb bombs. The first fell and exploded in a yard at the back of house No. 38, near Mr Melvin's coal yard, creating a crater 12 feet wide by 5 feet deep. The second one exploded in the dwelling house No. 28 Castle Street (now National Tyres & Autocare) which was completely demolished along with most of No. 30. The plane then flew off over the lower part of the town and the Toolworks and went out to sea. A number of people were trapped in the wrecked houses but all were released by 6.30pm. Eight people were killed including Mrs Mitchell and her daughter at No.28 and also Mrs Melvin at No. 30. A total of 29 men, women and children were also injured.

About 90 dwelling houses were damaged including No. 7 Duke Brae (Councillor Bob Stephen) and No. 9 (Mr Watt) and two were demolished. No air raid warning was given. This raid, like the one two months earlier on 19th February, was probably meant to hit Maconochie's Factory which was only about 200 yards further along Castle Street.

17th April 1941. Air raid at Castle Street.
Damage caused by bomb explosion at back of house No. 38 Castle Street.

17th April 1941.
Air raid at Castle St. showing houses Nos. 30 and 28, also in the background, right, Duke Brae houses Nos. 9 and 7.

20-4-1941 Air raid - Gut Factory, Marconi Road Houses and Toolworks

At 3.56pm on Sunday 20th April 1941, a low level attack was made on Fraserburgh by a German plane which came in from the east then wheeled around and, starting at the gut factory, dropped nine bombs in an easterly direction.

The first bomb exploded in the south east corner of the gut factory, the second at the edge of the accommodation road to the factory. Five were dropped in a grass field owned by the Philorth estates, another one on the boundary wall at the back of houses Nos. 98-102 Marconi Road and another between the gables of those properties. These bombs fell in a straight line over a distance of about 200 yards.

The plane then went south over the town and dropped two bombs in a grass field property of G. Benzie & Sons, Kirkton, about 150 yards south of the Toolworks. Ground defences opened fire. There were 10 casualties, none fatal, and about 45 properties were damaged. The 'alert' was sounded at 3.37pm.

4-6-1941 Air raid on Gut Factory and at Cairnbulg

At 3.08pm on the afternoon of 4th June 1941, a German plane approaching from the west made a low level attack by dropping 2 bombs on the gut factory. Then it passed over Kinnaird head and flew towards Cairnbulg.

One bomb exploded close to the outside of the north wall of the factory and about five yards from the base of the chimney stack. The other made a direct hit on the boiler house and exploded about five yards on the other side of the chimney stack. A boiler, 8 feet in diameter and 20 feet long, was blown out of the boiler house and landed on the edge of the first bomb crater outside the works. There were two casualties, neither serious. There was some machine gunning as the plane left the town causing 1 casualty.

Cairnbulg was then machine gunned at the watch hut, Whitelink Bay, but no damage or casualties occurred. There was no 'alert' until six minutes after the bombing. An unexploded cannon shell was found on the sea braes.

26-6-1941 Air raid on the Union Bank, now the Bank of Scotland

At 2.18am on Thursday morning 26th June 1941, a German plane passed over the town then turned around and made a low level attack by dropping two 1,000lb bombs. The first one fell in the garden at the rear of the Union Bank and house in Commerce Street making a large crater 51 feet in diameter and 20 feet deep. Mr Peter Brown, banker, his wife and her sister were asleep in the bank house and were trapped in the wreckage for a time until rescued, with no serious injury. The bank was severely damaged and unfortunately the beautiful pillared entry door where ARP personnel used to shelter when there was an 'alert' was completely destroyed. There was no 'alert' before that raid, and no air raid personnel were there. The second large bomb exploded in a garden area behind Nos. 17 and 19 Commerce Street and the TSB Bank in Broad Street. The house No. 17 was very badly damaged and, since that time, has been demolished and No. 19 (see photograph) has been rebuilt and improved. Both bombs left very large craters (see photograph) and caused extensive damage to about 260 buildings over a large area. On my way to work next morning, I saw stones and boulders in the street at College Bounds and Charlotte Street, about a quarter of a mile away. Casualties consisted of two killed and 17 injured several by large boulders falling thought the roofs of their houses.

Some particulars concerning the Union Bank - the entrance to the bank was at a curved corner from Seaforth Street round to Commerce Street and on four steps at the entry were four stone pillars supporting part of the upstairs flat which had windows from which could be seen a clear view of the harbour (see inset photograph). The whole magnificent building was very substantially built of Pitsligo granite.

At the back of the bank alongside Seaforth Street there was quite a large garden area consisting mostly of a large mound of earth with trees on top and it was at the end of the mound nearest the bank that the bomb fell. Considering the size of the building, the number of staff employed was very small. I can recollect seeing only the manager Peter Brown and Mr Chalmers, a clerk (now known as an accountant) being there.

Not long after the war it was taken over by the Bank of Scotland and eventually it was rebuilt as it stands today (see the photographs).

The Union Bank before the War.
Left hand photograph gives some idea of the height of the bank at the Corner of Commerce Street.
The right hand photograph shows the appearance of the bank and doorway with pillars as seen looking up from harbour.

26th June 1941.
The shattered Union Bank and bank house at the corner of
Commerce Street and Seaforth Street.

Air raid 26th June 1941.
Commerce Street, houses **LtoR**, Nos. 19, 21, 23, 25 and 27. The bomb crater was along from the Swan Café towards the TSB bank.

Air raid 26th June 1941.
The house No. 19 Commerce Street opposite the 'Justrite' shop and the bank. On the top right can just be seen Douglas Thomson, slater.

The Union Bank at the end of the war with a temporary office built on. Note the rounded corner with 4 steps up to the floor and, on the left, the only remaining pillar of four which supported the upper floor of the building. Part of the mound in the garden can be seen at the left.

The Union Bank taken over by the Bank of Scotland early in 1950 and repairs started.

7-9-1941 AIR RAID ALEXANDRA TCE AND OLD MATERNITY HOSPITAL

At 5 mins past 10pm on Sunday 7th September 1941, a high flying German plane cruised over Fraserburgh ('no alert') and dropped eight bombs; 7 across a field approximately where the present Academy is and the 8th in the middle of the old Dennyduff Road, just outside the old Maternity Hospital. I heard the bombs whistling down and ran for shelter, but there were no explosions. The seven unexploded bombs in the field were recovered by the disposal squad and destroyed at the sandhole near the golf course.

The eighth bomb in the middle of the road presented quite a problem for it fractured a 12" water main and soaked the ground and allowed the bomb to sink too far into the ground to be immediately recovered. The main was repaired and the hole filled with concrete as a temporary measure. Meantime the hospital patients were evacuated to Peterhead. There were no casualties. A little while later, a second attempt was made to recover the bomb but met with failure and it was covered up again. The third attempt, some time later, proved successful much to everybody's relief. The position of the bomb in present day terms would have been approximately near the Lochpots Road entrance to the present hospital.

This was the Maternity Hospital where, in the roadway outside, a bomb fell and penetrated a water main pipe without exploding. It sank so deep into the soggy ground that it took three attempts over many months before it could be extracted and destroyed at the sand hole near the golf course.

The hospital was earlier used as an 'isolation' hospital for patients with severe infectious diseases. Isolation in the early days meant far out of town on the 'old' Dennyduff Road (but now - the gateway would correspond with the entrance gate at the present hospital in Lochpots Road). Many mothers and grandmothers will remember this hospital. In the early 1900s, along the old road at the isolation hospital, on the right hand side, there were tennis courts for the use of the nurses.

14-11-1941 AIR RAID - OFF BROADSEA

At 12.46pm on Friday 14th November 1941, a German plane flew in from the south and attacked Fraserburgh by dropping bombs which were seen to pass over Maconochie's Factory and fall and explode in the sea close inshore between Broadsea Point and Kinnaird Head. There was no damage: nor were there casualties. The plane was estimated to be flying at between 1,500 and 2,000 feet and made several bursts of machine gun fire as it turned out seawards. It turned about again and passed over the south east part of the town where ground defences put up a heavy barrage. An air raid warning was given three minutes after the bombing.

14-2-1942 AIR RAID - BOMBS ON THE BEACH

At 7.48pm on Saturday 14th February 1942, a German plane was heard passing Fraserburgh over the sea near the coast after which it circled the town twice then flew south east passing approximately over the War Memorial. It then dropped three bombs which fell on the beach sands 250 yards south east of the pavilion and 400 yards east of the Toolworks. It is believed that the other two bombs fell and exploded in the sea. Damage was caused to glass and roof tiles at the pavilion and some damage to the houses 'St Modans' and 'Abbotsford', the alert was received seven minutes prior to the raid.

20-2-1943 AIR RAID - SCHOOL STREET & MID STREET

This was a raid that possibly took place as a consequence of an incident that occurred about two years earlier. After the War I was told by Major Charles Fraser, who was in command of the Home Guard, that one night early in the War he got a report that spies had been found up country west of Fraserburgh and he naturally wanted to know all about it. He tried to contact the police, but no matter how hard he tried, they would tell him nothing. He did find that British Intelligence Officials were dealing with it in secret, which made him feel very frustrated because, after all, he was head of the area's local defences.

Much later, after the War, the story came out that two Norwegians, 'John Moe' and 'Tor Glad' with radio and other equipment had been landed up the coast from a German submarine to be spies for the Germans. British Intelligence, however, persuaded them to act as double agents and they were installed at a safe house in Aberdeen from where they could transmit false or misleading information to Germany. It is possible that they did indeed influence the Germans in some way because the bombing in the Buchan area stopped for a whole year.

To keep up the deception 'Moe' sent a message requesting more money and radio gear and arranged for it to be dropped in the quiet area at Rattray lighthouse. A German plane duly arrived at about 2.30am on a clear morning on the 20th February 1943 and dropped a canister with their requirements. Instead of returning straight to their base, the German crew thought it a pity not to use some bombs on board, so they headed straight for Fraserburgh and, passing over the Hexagon, dropped four high explosive bombs on School Street at 2.48am on the 20th February, 1943.

The first bomb struck a 3-storey house with six tenants Nos. 91 to 101 School Street near its junction with Commerce Street, causing a great deal of damage at Commerce Street: it even broke the dial of the Central School clock.

The second bomb fell at the rear of and 60 feet from the tenement house with 6 tenants, Nos. 75 to 85.

The third bomb fell at the rear of and 21 feet from a 2-storey 4-tenanted house Nos. 57-61. A concrete air raid shelter was moved round 90^0. Luckily it was empty because the air raid alert was sounded too late for anyone to reach it.

(see photograph for fourth bomb description)

12- houses were so badly damaged that demolition was necessary.

13- houses were seriously damaged

376 - houses were slightly damaged

of other premises (shops etc)

3 - were totally demolished

3 - were seriously damaged

78 - were slightly damaged

Total of all properties damaged etc was 485.

Of the casualties, one eleven year old boy, Laurence Kerr, was killed in house No. 59. The spy, John Moe, was very disappointed about this raid and warned the Germans not to do it again. The Germans however did have another raid on 21st April 1943. See the report. It was the last raid.

20th February 1943.
School Street 1st Bomb.
Direct hit on a 3-storey flatted house,
tenants - Nos. 91 to 101.

20th February 1943. School Street fourth bomb.

As can be seen in the photograph this bomb caused the most damage - in the centre where 2 men are standing: Mr Bruce the Butcher's shop received a direct hit which destroyed the shop and everything in it. On the right of it, Mr Dillon Smith's Bakery Shop was also destroyed and some damage caused at a lane and yard further on. Mr and Mrs A. Main had a paper shop at the corner of School Street and Mid Street at the building on the left and were sleeping in the bedroom seen exposed in the picture. The floor of the room tilted over and they rolled down and landed on the rubble with no serious injury. Mr and Mrs George Watt were also sleeping in the same building and escaped with no serious injury. All around, buildings suffered damaged to roofs and windows.

The second and third bombs fell at School Street houses Nos. 75 to 85 and house Nos. 57 to 61. See text.

In this rather blurred picture, the men are trying to salvage some the 'Mains' goods.

22nd February 1943. School Street.
On Monday forenoon, two days after the bombing, Mr Dillon Smith, baker, on the left has set up a shop near his ruined shop and has resumed business. In the queue is the well known Norman Fordyce.

21 APRIL 1943 AIR RAID AT GREEN BANK & SMIDDYHILL THE LAST RAID AT FRASERBURGH

At 10.44pm on 21st April 1943, a German plane dropped nine bombs including some incendiaries, one of which failed to explode in grass and ploughed fields at Greenbank Croft, Smiddyhill and North Pitblae. Two people were injured, one of them Mrs McGregor who lived at Greenbank Cottage.

When she heard the noise of a plane flying over, she went to the front door and, just after she opened it, a bomb exploded in the field a few yards away. Mrs McGregor was struck on the head by a roof tile and she received medical attention at the first aid post.

A rather amusing story concerning the same place was told to me by Major Charles Fraser, Commander of the local home guard. When he went up next morning to see the damage at the cottage, he found two men at the bottom of the bomb crater poking at a yellowish fluid. He was immediately suspicious that the fluid might have had some connection with mustard gas which was a dangerous threat expected from the Germans, so he immediately had the men taken down to a decontamination centre at the Albert Street Toolworks factory where they were stripped and checked and fortunately found to be all clear. Window panes were broken by the blast in 11 houses in the town and at the isolation hospital.

Three other properties in the country district were also damaged.

Greenbank Cottage, Smiddyhill, which had its roof of the old type of red tiles shattered when a bomb exploded in the fields in front of the house. Incidentally - below the bushes flows the burn which filled the 'Watermill Dam' (no longer there) which supplied water to drive the waterwheel which turned the grinding stones in the meal mill.

29-1-1942 Air raids at Rosehearty

On the 29th January 1942, a German plane circled Rosehearty and dropped two bombs which demolished two houses and killed 11 women and children and injured seven. The plane then flew to Fraserburgh where it was driven off by heavy gun fire.

The people killed were:

Mrs Chalmers and her daughter Norma.
Mrs Noble and children George, William and Florence
and also an evacuee child.
Mrs Green and James Gunn
Miss Bruce and Miss Dorothy Duncan

There was also an earlier raid on 27th July 1940 when two bombs were dropped into the harbour without causing any damage (see report ref 'Toolworks').

Attacks on shipping at sea around the Fraserburgh area

This report is included in the book to let it be known that, although the people of Fraserburgh suffered a large number of casualties and damage from the bombing, the situation was as bad worse and as dangerous for the seamen in their ships at sea. Not only were they bombed and fired at, they were also torpedoed and had the uncertainty of striking mines and being blown up.

Convoys of cargo boats coming round Kinnaird Head and moving south were particularly vulnerable to air attack. This I know something about because one afternoon, in broad daylight, I joined a crowd of C.P. toolworkers on the beach prom, where we watched a convoy of ships crossing the bay towards Cairnbulg Point suffering a heavy attack by low flying German bombers. The planes were circling around the convoy and we got quite a fright when one came over the prom. The pilot was too busy to notice us however but I am sure that the seamen were having a horrible time.

It is a pity that there was no sign of any 'Spitfires' joining the battle because they were the only fighter planes that the Germans were afraid of. When you read the following extracts from reports you will understand better what I mean by the dangers at sea.

Short extracts from reports of ships etc involved

3-1-1940 At about 8.00am the cargo ship 'SS Svarton', 2,460 gross tons was on passage from Narvik to Middlesbrough with a cargo of iron ore and when 9½ miles N.E. of Kinnaird Head it was either torpedoed or struck a mine and sank within a minute. The crew jumped overboard and 40 minutes later eleven survivors were picked up by the admiralty trawler 'H.M.S. Oak', transferred to the Fraserburgh Lifeboat and landed at Fraserburgh about 11.30am.

The survivors were six Swedes and five Norwegians and missing were 11 Swedes and nine Norwegians.

❖

2-2-1940 At 8.35am Fraserburgh lifeboat received a call to search for survivors of the Swedish Ship the 'S.S.

Fram' which had been sunk about one mile from the New Aberdour coast. Five of the crew were picked up by the Aberdeen trawler 'Viking Deep' 10 miles north of Troup Head and were landed at Macduff. From them it was learned that 19 men and one woman were missing. The lifeboat found no trace of any other survivors and returned home.

❖

24-3-1940 The H.M. Trawler 'Loch Assater' (A 321) was sunk by two mines in the North Sea and the whole crew of 13 members were picked up by the H.M.T. 'Strath Tummel' (A 402) and landed at Fraseburgh at about 11.30am. Three of the crew, including the skipper, were stretcher cases and all received attention at the first aid post before being transferred to Kingseat Naval Hospital. The trawler was on patrol about 70 miles N.E. half N. off Fraserburgh when it was sunk.

❖

3-4-1940 At about midday the 'S.T. Delilah' (A 182) carrying a cargo of fish from the Shetland Isles to Aberdeen was attacked by two Heinkel bombers when 35 miles NNW of Kinnaird Head. They circled the trawler then dropped a number of HE bombs and incendiaries and some aerial torpedoes, and then machine gunned her. Two incendiary bombs landed on the foredeck but were extinguished. The attack lasted about half an hour but there were no injuries.

❖

17-7-1941 At about 2.00pm two fishermen, Thomas Third of Main Street Cairnbulg and his son Robert of 27 Saltoun Place, Fraserburgh, were fishing 1½ miles N.E. off Cairnbulg in their boat MB 'Speedwell' (FR 306) when they saw men in a yellow rubber boat waving to them. In the boat they found four hungry German airmen one of whom was wounded and they said that a fifth member had been drowned when their plane sank. They were taken on to the fishing boat and, towing the rubber boat, were landed at Fraserburgh from where they were taken away for interview.

❖

24-9-1940 At about 1.40am the 77 ton steam trawler 'Northward' (GY 110) of Grimsby ran on the rocks immediately north of Cairnbulg Beacon. Their echometer was out of order due to a mine explosion some weeks earlier but not yet repaired. The crew were taken off by breeches-buoy and taken to Fraserburgh.

❖

29-9-1940 At 8.00pm the 4814 gross tons cargo ship the SS 'Queen City' of Bedford with 45 crew members and carrying 7860 tons of steel from Montreal to Middlesbrough in convoy with 14 other ships was attacked 25 miles north of Troup Head by enemy bombers. The ship was struck by HE and incendiary bombs causing great damage and starting a fire. The ship was abandoned with the crew in two lifeboats - 15 in one boat were picked up and taken to Fraserburgh by the Fraserburgh Lifeboat and the others picked up by the H.M.S. Minesweeper L.207. Another boat was believed to have been struck and sunk.

❖

30-10-1940 There is a report that the Fraserburgh first aid post had attended to 172 ship-wrecked seamen but no details are given.

8-10-1940 In the afternoon of 8th October, four St. Combs fishermen Andrew Buchan and David Buchan of 5 Braeheads, James Buchan, 11 Gordon Street, and John Buchan, Corskelly Place, were fishing in their two motor yawls one mile north of Rattray Head when they saw a German plane flying low fall into the sea about 50 yards offshore. They immediately pulled their lines and went to the rescue. Andrew and David took one airman off the plane and James and John picked up two men trying to swim ashore. They were then taken to Fraserburgh for interrogation by the intelligence.

❖

8-10-1940 About 8.00pm when a Danish ship the S.S. 'Bellona' was leading a convoy northwards off the Kincardineshire coast going from Hull to Iceland it was attacked and caught fire followed by explosions. About 10.00pm the same night the skipper of the Grimsby Trawler (GY 485) heard shouting from someone in the water whom he rescued and took into Fraserburgh. The survivor was put on to a train to Stonehaven where he joined the remainder of the crew.

❖

1-3-1941 The Aberdeen stream trawler 'St Agnes No.1 (SN 88), skipper Frederick Wm. White, left Fraserburgh harbour at 11.30am and, when 22 miles NW by N off Kinnaird Head, was attacked and a bomb or aerial torpedo passed right through the wheelhouse from starboard to port killing the mate William S. West (37) 63 Victoria Road and Issac Johnston (58) deckhand, 43 Cotton Street, both from Aberdeen. A second bomb exploded aft of the boat. The rest of the crew were below deck and no one saw the raider. The boat returned to Fraserburgh where Dr Wilson and an ambulance were in attendance.

❖

8-4-1941 At about 3.00pm the motor boat 'Reward' (FR I53) under the charge of Peter Tait (54), skipper, 12 Main Street, Cairnbulg, with James Duthie Masson (14), 12 Main Street, was returning to Fraserburgh and when 1½ miles from Kinnaird Head they were attacked by a low flying plane which machine gunned the boat, then circled and flew off. No one was injured but one bullet struck the boat.

❖

9-4-1941 At about 10.30pm two patrol boats H.M.T. 'Annabelle' and H.M.T. 'Cloughstone' were attacked 4 miles off Rattray Head by a plane flying about mast high which dropped 4 HE bombs on the 'Annabelle' the last one of which was so close that it threw the trawler upwards causing damage to the engine room and cabin fittings. It also machine gunned the boat and was replied by a burst of fire from the boat's gun. The plane returned again and dropped two bombs the second one so close to the 'Cloughstone' that it sprang a leak and damaged the engine. The 'Annabelle' then towed the 'Cloughstone' to Fraserburgh Harbour. There were no casualties.

❖

7-9-1941 About 11.00pm the cargo boat 'SS Frsat', 1,369 tons gross of Swansea was attacked seven miles off Kinnaird Head. A number of bombs were dropped one of which struck the foredeck and caused so much damage that the boat sank shortly afterwards. A lifeboat was launched, but most of the crew jumped into the sea. One of the crew was killed, two were missing and the remaining 14 were rescued by the Fraserburgh lifeboat and taken to the First Aid post for attention and medical treatment.

The Fraserburgh gut factory which seemed to be a favourite target for the German Bombers for it was attacked several times.

'George Cross' Hero.
Mr John Forbes was an enemy aircraft spotter at a post on the beach prom for C.P.T when he heard the sound of an explosion in a Mine field at the sandhole. He ran across, saw 3 young girls inside, went straight in and picked up a wounded one and took them to safety. The injured one unfortunately died later. For this brave act he was awarded the George Cross.

The Fraserburgh Volunteer Police during the 2nd War. **L to R.**
Back Row: Wm. Flett, Andrew Henderson, Wm. Bruce, Wm. Mc Hardy, Chas. McLean, Geo. Henderson, Dod Milne.
2nd Row: Bert Gordon, McWillie, Andrew Stephen, Wm. Walker, Bobby Cooper, D. Gordon, Tom Allison, Chas. West, Dod Melvin,
Chas. Noble, ?, ?
3rd Row: A. Carlaw, D. Anderson, Jeans, Alf Russell, Bruce Kemp, Wm. Maitland, Louis Birnie, C. Cardno,
W. Craigie, B. Mitchell, Henderson.
Front Row: 1. ? Norman Simpson, John Strachan, Chas. McBain, Isaac Dunbar, Alex Bruce, C. Cheyne,
D. Rothney, D. Chalmers, A. Christie.

Some of the Volunteer Fire Brigade, Fraserburgh C. 1940.
Back Row: Cowe, A. Bruce, J. Esslemont, A. Crawford, A. Bruce, J. Buchan
Second Back: A. Taylor, J. Murison, J. Taylor, George Campbell, G. Sinclair, A. Davidson, G. Watt, A. Bruce, L. Murison
Seated: A. Mair, Birrel, W. Elrick, I. Cowan
Front: A. McNab, J. Rufford, A. Shirron, G. Burnet, ?, F. Buchan

These girls were taking part in a parade of 'Floats' in 1941 collecting money for 'Wings for Victory' in which they had the winning float.
These girls were taking part in a parade of 'Floats' in 1941 collecting money for 'Wings for Victory' in which they had the winning float.
They were from a large group of 'trainees' directed from all over Aberdeenshire to the C.P.T. Factory for War work, mostly for Rolls
Royce Engines. In the picture: **L to R** - G. Rodger, Elsie Smith (lorry driver) E. Angus, M. Scott, N. Young (Sim), K. Stephen (Tait), Mrs
Stephen (McKenzie), J. McIntosh and Betty Anderson.

The C.P.T. factory - an important target for the German bombers because of the vital components produced there.

1943. Members of the No.1383 squadron of the Air Training Corps and Scouts invited to see the film 'Coastal Command' at the High Street cinema. Seated at the front were Air Commodore Spence and Provost Thomson, Mr McTaggart (cinema manager) and squadron leader Mr J.B. McDonald officers and personnel (starting behind Provost Thomson), Mr Pressley, Eddie Lamb (bugle) F.O. Charlie Grant, Billie Lamb (drum), F.O. Bob Ferguson, Charlie Clark (bugle), F.O. Andrew Linklater and F.O. George A Dey. In the far right hand end of back row is Mr. Peter Christie signals instructor.

The No. 1383 squadron of the Air Training Corps was formed in May 1941, the object to train young men for quick entry into the RAF and initially about 70 men joined and received training in engineering and signalling etc. Shooting was not part of the training but, somehow, the squadron leader Flight Lieutenant John B. McDonald had acquired some ammunition and made an arrangement with the New Aberdour Home Guard to have a shooting competition at their range across a valley not far from the beach. I have been told that the ammunition came from a Wellington bomber which had gone off its course from Aberdeen and crashed on Beinn A-Bhuird, a 3,922 feet high mountain a few miles north west of Braemar. Mr McDonald was well known in the Braemar area for the wonderful films he produced of the 'games' and deer stalking, and no doubt but he got lots of local help collecting the ammunition. Two airmen were killed in the crash and three died later on active service.

Regarding the shooting competition, Fraserburgh, A.T.C. won by a small margin and one of the lads had the 'honour' of a direct hit on the sticky paste bottle used for patching the target between rounds.
In the picture are: **L to R**
Pilot Officer George Dey, Flight Lieut. John B. McDonald, Jack Mclean, Sandy Bruce and Alan Scott.
Front row: F. Ritchie, Jim Crockett, D. Gordon and Peter Christie, (signals instructor).

When the Germans started dropping 'magnetic mines' in the convoy routes, many steel constructed ships passing over them or near them attracted a magnetic device which caused the mine to explode. An all wooden type of minesweeper was quickly designed in which Mr Forbes of Sandhaven was involved and, from the drawings, these boats were built in all available shipyards around the country. The one in the picture was built at Noble's Yard at Fraserburgh. The scientists also devised an electrical system called 'Degausing' which rendered the mines harmless. A large drum of special cable can be seen at the stern of the ship for minesweeping.

Large steel ships were later fitted with degausing cables all round from stem to stern as protection against the mines.

The Duke of Kent speaks to members of the crew of Fraserburgh lifeboat 14th July, 1939. Making the presentations (right) is Provost Thomson. The crew (from the left) 1st Andrew Ritchie, 2nd ?, 3rd Rory Johnston and 4th the Coxswain Davie Hay.

On board the motor drifter 'Faithful' at Fraserburgh harbour. From the left is Provost Thomson, Skipper William Whyte and the Duke of Kent. 14th July 1939.

13 December 1943: Sir Stafford Cripps, Minister of Aircraft Production, addressed a meeting of some of the workers at the Consolidated Pneumatic Toolworks Factory which was deeply involved in producing parts for the war effort.
Some people identified in the group - **L to R**: Billie Lamb, Nan Young, Charlie Watt, Bill Summers, L.D. Ritchie, Jim Crockett and J. Buchan, Others believed to be in the picture are Mrs. Simpson, G. Craig, C. Murdoch, Miss Ritchie, Madge Ritchie, Stan Stephen, Bob Rendall, Phemy Cahoone, Miss Young.

On December 13th, 1943 Sir Stafford Cripps toured the C.P.T. Co. Factory and is seen bending over and watching Geo. Whyte delicately assembling baked sand cores into a sand moulding. Beside him is Mr J.U. Vass, manager of the factory, and on the right is Mr Howard Bird, a director from the American parent company.

During World War II The Consolidated Pneumatic Toolworks was very heavily involved, day and night, in 3 factories making tools and compressors, as well as complete units for Rolls Royce Merlin engines and parts for 'Bofors' guns. For use in aeroplane construction factories many thousands of small eighth HP Pneumatic Drills - straight and with angular heads for use in difficult places - were made and used as in the picture. The drill pictured above was designed by the author.

On V.J Day (Victory over Japan)

As part of the celebrations some fishing boats took members of the public on trips around Fraserburgh Bay. On the 'Margaret Rose'. **L to R** are Helen Malley, Kathleen Dey and Jean Johnston.

V.J Day, 13th Aug 1945 Victory in the War Against Japan

I can remember very little about the celebrations for they were very subdued compared with those on V.E. Day but I do remember that it was a fine sunny day - all the better for the fishing boat trips from the harbour - and last but not least the bonfire in the late evening. This was quite a large, built just beyond the 'flag pole' and had in its base some barrels of tar on top of which were piled all sorts of inflammable material.

Suddenly, when it was well alight with a large crowd of people around it, there was a big explosion and burning material was scattered all around injuring a number of people and children who were really too close to it. Many onlookers ran off home and the injured were attended to by the first aid people. The explosion was caused by the bursting of the tar barrels due to the excessive heat around them.

'CORONATION'

CORONATION CELEBRATIONS
at FRASERBURGH
2nd JUNE 1953

The Town Council members, being determined to make sure that the Fraserburgh celebrations would be memorable for everyone, young and old, held meetings with all organisations and traders to prepare a suitable programme of events.

The first thing to do of course was to arrange a public meeting in the square in order to offically proclaim the forthcoming Coronation (see first photograph). They then arranged a comprehensive programme of events as follows:-

A few days before the Coronation, the children in the schools were to be told about it and, provided they took their ration books with them, they were to be given a supply of chocolate.

On the morning of 2nd June the celebrations were to start with a parade of all the youth organisations from the Links at 9.00am to attend a service in the South Church.

During the morning there was to be a twenty-one gun salute at the playing fields performed by members of the Local Royal Artillery under the command of Captain Jack Herd - at a cost of £15.00.

All people, young and old, in fancy dress and decorated floats had to be in Albert Street ready for the judges at 1.00pm and then they would start the parade through the town at 1.30pm.

In the afternoon, there was to be a picnic and sports at the playing fields for all children during which they would be given a bag of cakes and a bottle of lemonade.

In the evening at 10.30pm there was to be a bonfire and fireworks display and the C.P.T. Toolworks was to be illuminated with a display of colour lighting.

Well, the great day came and what a disappointment! It was pouring rain and there were gale force winds so the councillors quickly changed all their "best laid schemes" and tried to make things more comfortable for all concerned.

The youth organisations parade started from King Edward Street at 9.00am and, under the command of Lieut. Breen of the Sea Cadets, they all marched down Victoria Street led by the British Legion Pipe Band straight to the South Church.

In the church were assembled members of the Town Council, Lieut. Gommander McLean-Foreman and men from the minesweeper in the harbour, the Feuars Managers, the Harbour Commissioners and the ladies of the Townswomen's Guild.

The minister of the church, Rev. R. F. Howat, led the service assisted by the Rev. F.M. Hirst of St. Peters Church and the Rev. A. M. Munro of the Congregational Church.

At the end of the service, the organisations were quickly lined up and marched to the War Memorial.

At about 10.00am the twenty-one gun salute took place.

Meantime, the fancy dress parade and floats were lined up, judged and moved off about at 12 o'clock via Charlotte Street and Broad Street to the Links near the South Church.

The Prize Winners were:

> **Tableaux** 1st, Benzie & Miller; 2nd, Towns Women Guild, Queen Victoria; 3rd, Mary Queen of Scots, Special Prize Queen Elizabeth.
>
> **Trade** 1st, Consolidated Toolworks was also the best overall entry; 2nd, Nobles Dairy; 3rd, Gordon & Sampson's Herring Display; Special - Scottish Gas Board.
>
> **Sports** 1st, Fraserburgh Amateur Swimming Club; 2nd, Tennis Club; 3rd, Football Club; Special - Fraserburgh Commercial for Horse & Lorry Turnout.
>
> Prizes were given to all children.

The 'Portable House' was supposed to contain 'Jane Russell' and 'Marilyn Monroe'. 'Wallace Dairy' had a massive crown, 'Ship Repairing Co. was commended as also was 'A.L. McDonald's' lovely permanent waved models.

The Judges were:
> **Tableux** Mr and Mrs George Bremner Walker
> **Trades** Lieut. Commander McLean-Foreman, Capt. Duthie and Mr J. Mitchell
> **Fancy Dress** Mr Sydney Burnett and Mr Duthie (Art Teachers)

The playing field events for the children were cancelled and instead they were divided into three groups, one each to the High Street and Mid Street cinemas where they were entertained by comedy film shows and the third group went to the Dalrymple Hall where they were entertained by the 'Burnett's' and the 'Boyndlie" 'dancers. All the children received their bag of "goodies" and ice-cream.

The bonfire and fireworks display and C.P.T. Illuminations were carried out as planned.

At Fraserburgh 1953. The Proclamation of Queen Elizabeth's accession to the throne.
In the picture **left to right**:

Robert Stephen, Rev. Clarkson (West Church), Rev. Muir (Rosehearty), Rev. A. Mitchell (Old Parish), Provost H. Milne, (behind him, head only, is J. Boyle, Town Clerk), Louis Pressley (trumpeter), Alex R. Noble, J. Wiseman, A. Benzie (of B&M), Magnus Robertson

Lined up in Albert Street.
This is part of the 1953 parade with exhibits showing some of the trades and activities in the town.

Firemen enjoying a break and hoping that the rain won't spoil their bonny extending ladder machine.
Members **L. to R.** George Watt, Alex. Sim, and Alex. Crawford.
All "Laughing in the Rain".

Football Team - mostly C.P.T. Co. Players. 1953.
standing: Duncan Will, Albert Cruden, Ivor Robertson, James Bain, Farquhar Muirhead
kneeling: Bertie Fraser, Gordon Russell (with Challenge Cup), Gilbert Duthie, Andy Watt
on road: Mr Muirhead (father of Farquhar), Tom Tinley, Jerry Murison
3rd Prize in "Sports" section.

Waiting for the parade to start, a rather cold looking 'Fairy', a fierce looking 'Rob Roy'and a hopeful winner of the 'Buchan Firkin'.

The parade participants include:
Ena Tait, Vic Revalles and, on cycle, A. Bowman and beside him young Miss Cassie.

The men on this 'float' are demonstrating the drilling of holes into a block of Kemnay granite, the hardest available. The man on top is using a hand held rock drill and the other two are using pneumatic air support legs which push the rock drills forward into the rock. At that time the drills were capable of drilling at a rate of about 12 inches per minute but before the factory closure drills were developed at Fraserburgh capable of drilling 22 to 24 inches per minute. They were very powerful and noisy and required the operators to wear ear-muffs. In the centre is Bob Adams and looking on is Chief Test Engineer, Steve Johnston.
The display was placed first in the Trades Section
and first in the whole parade.

On the lorry is one of the Toolworks' largest compressors, capable of supplying 600 cubic feet of air compressed per minute to 100lbs per square inch and driven by a 120 horse power engine. The air is being piped to a demonstration "float".

In Seaforth Street - moving house with a police escort.

Members of Benzie and Miller's staff seem to be enjoying modelling sports clothing in spite of the rain.
In the picture:
Marian Livingstone (Lawrence), Marian Sim (Duthie), Margaret Milne and Irene Murdoch (Mair).This was 1st prize winner in the
Tableaux Section and was probably designed by Andrew Cardno.

The 'Queen' looks rather unsafe on top of 'B & M's' lorry.

Members of the Sea Swimming Club making it obvious that there was a need for a larger swimming pool.
Their wish was granted a few years later.
On the float were:
Stella Morrice, Cathie Bruce, James Hendry, Alex Simpson, Ian Eddie, Charlie Thom, Margaret Buchan and Catherine Munro.
This was a first prize winning entry in the 'Sports' Section.

Nessie Birnie and Doreen Sim getting ready for a trip pulled by the speedboat "Roamer".

Doreen Sim and Nessie Birnie now on their way. There were no wet suits in 1953.
They deserved a special prize for bravery.

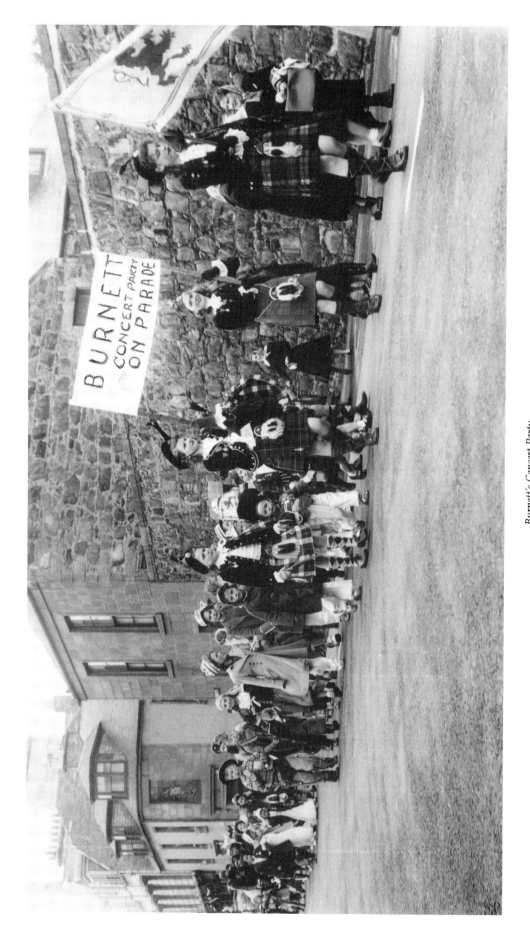

Burnett's Concert Party.
Mary Simpson (May), Alixa Burnett (Gunn), Helen Green (Duthie),
Derek Walker, June McIntosh (Ritchie), Sandra Duff.

Many good costumes in the children's part of the parade. Some of you will remember the song - 'How much is that Doggie in the Window?'

Picture House staff in action as they pass the Dalrymple Hall. Projectionist - John Craighead, assisted by John Watt.

A display by the Fraserburgh Tennis Club.
This was a Second Prize winning entry in the 'Sports' Section.

At the end of their journey.
Wet and still cheerful.

At the rear of the parade.
O.A.P.'s in a decorated bus with pictures of the Royal family on the windows.

As part of the celebrations there was a Twenty One gun salute in the morning in pouring rain at the Fraserburgh playing fields carried out by the members of the Royal Artillery commanded by Captain Jack Herd. The cost of the operation was £15.00.

At approx. 9.30am on the 2nd June, 1953.
Leading the parade into the South Church were the Provost & Town Council members, the Feuars Managers, the Harbour Commissioners and other V.I.P. representatives of the town.
From the right:- at the edge of the picture, Robert A. Slessor, Sergeant Charles Ingram, Inspector Tom Cruickshank, Lieut. Commander McLean-Foreman (from the minesweeper at the harbour), Provost Harold Milne, James Boyle (Town Clerk), Alex. Noble, Wm. Benzie (of B & M's) and amongst the people behind, Wm. Kennedy (Academy Rector) and J. Wiseman.

In this picture are pipers:
Fraser Murison, Doig, Sandy Fraser, G. Fraser and Leslie Fraser.

After the Church Service the organisations start to re-assemble.

The parade is now ready to move off commanded by Lieut. Breen of the Sea Cadets seen standing in front of the bus.

Tuning up ready for "quick march".
In this picture are drummers Charlie Allan, J. Fraser and G. Leslie.

Never mind the rain
Here we are again.
The parade moves off.

Leading the Fraserburgh Pipe Band from the South Church is the well known Fraser Murison on the extreme right.
Pipers in the front row are, in centre, Charlie Christie, and on each side of him the brothers Fraser.

The Sea Cadets.
Some members: Ian Bremner, Sandy Massie, Eddie Lillie, Alan Eddie and Robert Tait.

The Army Cadets led by Louis Smith (son of "Ginger" Smith). Others: Geo. Skinner, John Campbell and 'Caley'.

No. 1383 Squadron of the Air Training Corps. Led by Commanding Officer Bob Ferguson, followed by F. Tocher. Others are Geo. Ironside and Mr Rankine. Aren't they smart!

1953 Girls Nautical Training Corp.
Leading is Miss Cairns
Girls: Hilary Ross, Miss Swanson, Jessie Bellamy, Pat Summers, Miss McDonald, Elisha McIntosh, Jean Coutts (McHardy), Pamela Duthie. Taking it seriously!

The Girls Training Corps. led by Miss Bain.
Others in the picture:-
Elma Robertson, Mabel Trail (Sinclair), Grace Strachan, Ena Lawrence and Bessie Webster (Campbell).
Aren't they lovely!

A toolworker called 'Ironside' stands on guard outside the Consolidated Pneumatic offices during the 'E.R.' celebrations.

Decorations and coloured illuminations outside the Consolidated Pneumatic Toolworks with, standing at the front, lifesize figures representing members of the forces.

For the Coronation celebrations Messrs Benzie and Miller had an ingenious display on the roof of their partly re-built store in Mid Street after it was destroyed by a disastrous fire during a German bombing raid on the 5th Nov. 1940.

On the roof are two large model boats, one marked 'E.R. 1953' and a model fort with soldiers standing guard at the front. This display was designed and set up by Andrew Cardno, a superb window dresser who won many prizes for B & M and other shops in Fraserburgh with his attractive displays against nation wide competition.

These two pictures show part of the Coronation display on the roof of Messrs. Benzie and Miller's large store in which were sold all kinds of household goods and dresswear.

On the 5th November 1940, the original shop was destroyed by a disastrous fire. The glare of the fire made Fraserburgh a target for a German bombing raid which caused much damage and killed many people.